FORENSICS: THE SCENE OF THE CRIME

Lynn Peppas

CRABTREE
Publishing Company
www.crabtreebooks.com

Crabtree Publishing Company
www.crabtreebooks.com

Author: Lynn Peppas
**Publishing plan research
    and development**: Reagan Miller
Editors: Sonya Newland, Kathy Middleton
Proofreader: Crystal Sikkens
Photo Researcher: Sonya Newland
Original design: Tim Mayer
    (Mayer Media)
Book design: Tim Mayer
Cover design: Ken Wright
**Production coordinator and
    prepress tecnician**: Ken Wright
Print coordinator: Katherine Bertie

Produced for Crabtree Publishing
Company by White-Thomson Publishing

Cover Artist: Dorling Kindersley RF

Photographs:
Alamy: ZUMA Press, Inc.: pp. 35, 41
Corbis: Ted Soqui/Sygma: pp. 10–11;
Bettmann: p. 19; Neal Preston: pp. 44–45
Getty Images: pp. 15, 30, 36–37, 38–39
Press Association Images: Ricardo Brazziell/
AP: pp. 32–33
Shutterstock: Corepics VOF: pp. 1, 13; Johan
Swanepoel: p. 7; mikeledray: pp. 8–9; Shots
Studio: p. 14; tanewpix: p. 16; Leah-Anne
Thompson: p. 17; kilukilu: p. 21; Dale A
Stork: pp. 24, 34; isak55: pp. 30–31; Kevin L
Chesson: pp. 42–43
SuperStock: Cultura Limited: p. 5; Fancy
Collection: p. 6; Imagebroker.net: pp. 20, 28–
29; Jochen Tack/imagebroker.net: pp. 22–23
Thinkstock: JaysonPhotography: p. 12; James
Ferrie: p. 18; Digital Vision: p. 25; 36 Clicks: p.
26; Nicholas Monu: p. 27; roberthyrons: p. 40 .

Library and Archives Canada Cataloguing in Publication

Peppas, Lynn, author
    Forensics : the scene of the crime / Lynn Peppas.

(Crabtree chrome)
Includes index.
Issued in print and electronic formats.
ISBN 978-0-7787-1363-0 (bound).--ISBN 978-0-7787-1399-9 (pbk.).--
ISBN 978-1-4271-8979-0 (pdf).--ISBN 978-1-4271-8973-8 (html)

    1. Forensic sciences--Juvenile literature. I. Title. II. Series:
Crabtree chrome

HV8073.8.P47 2014   j363.25   C2014-903926-3
                                        C2014-903927-1

Library of Congress Cataloging-in-Publication Data

Peppas, Lynn.
    Forensics : the scene of the crime / Lynn Peppas.
        pages cm. -- (Crabtree chrome)
    Includes index.
    ISBN 978-0-7787-1363-0 (reinforced library binding) --
ISBN 978-0-7787-1399-9 (pbk.) -- ISBN 978-1-4271-8979-0
(electronic pdf) -- ISBN 978-1-4271-8973-8 (electronic html)
    1. Forensic sciences--Juvenile literature. I. Title.

HV8073.8.P46 2015
363.25--dc23

2014022781

Crabtree Publishing Company
www.crabtreebooks.com   1-800-387-7650

Printed in the U.S.A./092014/JA20140811

Published in Canada
Crabtree Publishing
616 Welland Ave.
St. Catharines, ON
L2M 5V6

Published in the United States
Crabtree Publishing
PMB 59051
350 Fifth Avenue, 59th Floor
New York, New York 10118

Published in the United Kingdom
Crabtree Publishing
Maritime House
Basin Road North, Hove
BN41 1WR

Published in Australia
Crabtree Publishing
3 Charles Street
Coburg North
VIC 3058

Contents

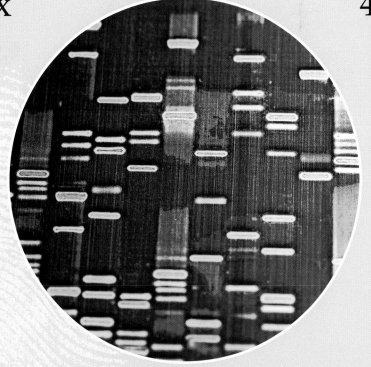

Forensic Discoveries

A Murder Mystery

In 1995, the body of a young woman was discovered lying beside a river in Utah. Police investigators found the rock that crushed the young woman's skull, but little other evidence. For almost 20 years, her murder went unsolved. Then, in 2013, investigators heard about a new kind of vacuum developed to remove bacteria from food.

The U.S. Federal Bureau of Investigation (FBI) established the world's first forensic crime laboratory in 1932. Today, more than 500 forensic experts work there, using cutting-edge science and technology to solve crimes.

▶ *Forensic scientists are among the first people called to the scene of a crime.*

Solving Cold Cases

Scientists used the new M-Vac vacuum on the bloody rock. It picked up DNA evidence that matched the DNA on a cigarette thrown away by a suspect. The murderer was convicted almost two decades after the crime. Figuring out what really happened to victims of crimes—sometimes many years afterward—is the fascinating job of **forensic** scientists.

forensic: a scientific way to solve a crime

Early Autopsies

You might think that forensics is a new type of science, but people have been using forensic science to solve crimes for centuries. One of the first people to write down his methods was a doctor in China named Song Ci. He wrote a book around 1200 CE on how to perform autopsies to help **investigate** crimes.

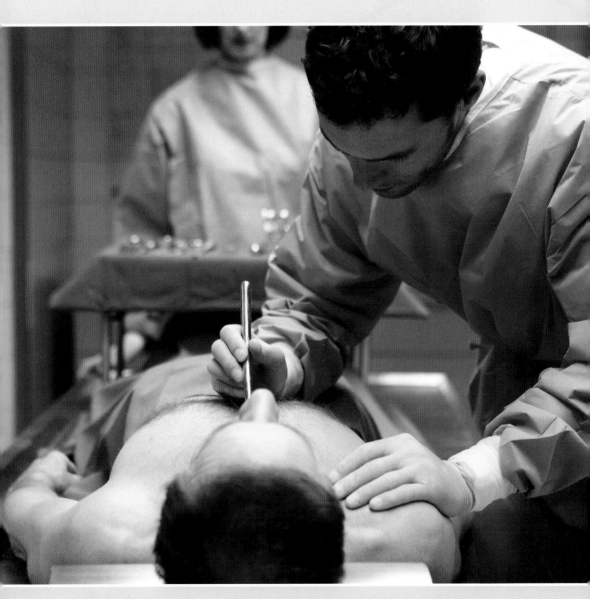

▲ *An autopsy is the examination of a body to try to find the cause of death. It is usually carried out by a doctor called a pathologist.*

Fingerprint Evidence

Fingerprints were first used to solve a crime more than 100 years ago. In 1892, in Buenos Aires, Argentina, a woman's children were murdered in their home. The woman accused her neighbor of the crime. An officer found a bloody fingerprint at the crime scene—and matched it to the children's mother. She confessed to the murders.

▶ *In the 1880s, English scientist Francis Galton created a system to classify fingerprints. The system is still used today.*

In 1880, Scottish doctor Henry Faulds noticed how the pattern of fingerprints sometimes stayed on surfaces. He also realized that everyone's fingerprints were different. His discovery led to the widespread use of identification through fingerprinting.

investigate: look into something to discover the truth

CROSS   SHERIFF'S LINE DO NOT CROSS   SHERIFF'S LINE

The Beginnings of Forensics

In 1889, French professor Alexandre Lacassagne was the first to study bullets. He examined the markings left on a bullet after it was fired. He discovered that these markings could be traced back to a particular gun. This field of science became known as **ballistics**. In 1920, a colonel in the U.S. Army, Calvin Goddard, developed a special microscope that allowed an even closer look at the markings.

Trace Evidence

Edmond Locard was an important early forensic scientist. In the late 1800s, Locard was the first to look at trace evidence. Trace evidence is a clue such as an extremely small fiber, hair, paint chip, or other fragment left at the scene of a crime. Locard set up the world's first forensic laboratory in France in 1910.

◀ *By studying bullets, their casings, or coverings, and holes left by bullets, scientists can tell which type of gun was used and where the shooter was standing.*

Locard said that "every contact leaves a trace." This means that every person at the scene of a crime brings something to it— and takes something away. This is known as "Locard's Exchange Principle."

ballistics: the scientific study of bullets and firearms

Forensics at Work

Keeping the Scene Clean

Forensic scientists start their work at the scene of the crime. This is where the evidence trail usually begins. It is important that the scene is not disturbed before they get there. The people who discovered the crime, police officers, and emergency responders, must all be very careful not to **contaminate** the crime scene.

The O.J. Simpson Trial

Football legend O.J. Simpson was accused of murdering his ex-wife Nicole and another person at her home in 1994. When the case went to court, Simpson's lawyers were able to show that some of the DNA evidence had been collected and handled improperly. It cast enough doubt on the DNA evidence that Simpson was found "not guilty" of the murders.

"Untrained officers trampled ... through the evidence. Because of their bungling, they ignored the obvious clues. They didn't pick up paper at the scene with prints on it."

O.J. Simpson's lawyer, explaining that police had ignored evidence that would have led to a different suspect

◄ Simpson's mishandled blood sample led his lawyer to accuse police of planting Simpson's blood at the crime scene.

contaminate: change something so it is no longer reliable evidence

Handle with Care!

Crime scene investigators (CSIs) protect evidence by "securing" a crime scene. Around the area, they put bright yellow tape with black lettering. Police officers guard the crime scene. Everyone involved in the search for evidence wears protective clothing such as **latex** gloves, booties over their shoes, hair coverings, overalls, and masks.

▲ *Crime scenes are sealed off so that members of the public cannot get too close.*

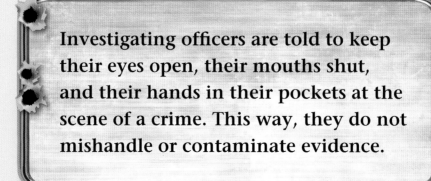

Investigating officers are told to keep their eyes open, their mouths shut, and their hands in their pockets at the scene of a crime. This way, they do not mishandle or contaminate evidence.

Recording Evidence

All details from the crime scene are carefully written down or recorded. Investigators take photographs and may make video recordings. Sometimes, the investigation requires a "fingertip search." This means crawling over every inch of a crime scene in search of evidence.

▼ *Possible evidence is marked with paper labels or small flags.*

latex: a material from plants that is used to make a type of rubber

Criminalists

The scientists who collect evidence at a crime scene are called criminalists. Criminalists run basic tests on evidence in forensic laboratories. They use their findings to explain how an accident or crime happened. Sometimes, experts who specialize in one field of forensics are called in. They might specialize in dental forensics—drawing conclusions from teeth or bite patterns. Or they might be specialists in digital forensics, finding clues in computers or cell phones.

▲ *Anthropology is a specialized forensic science that deals with the study of bones found at crime scenes.*

Collecting and Explaining Data

Forensic scientists may enter their findings in data-collection programs. These programs sometimes match evidence from a crime scene with criminals who have committed crimes in the past. Criminalists may go to court during a trial, to talk about their findings and answer any questions.

▼ Forensic **animation** is often used in court to demonstrate how a crime could have taken place.

Forensic animation uses computer graphics to recreate a crime. Criminalists analyze evidence and explain their findings to an animator. The animator creates a cartoon-like video of the crime, which can be used in court.

animation: pictures or graphics that seem to show movement

Types of Evidence

The Importance of Evidence

In 1990, the wife of a wealthy business owner was murdered in Colorado. An Arizona man saw the case on the TV show *Unsolved Mysteries* and told the police that his brother-in-law had confessed to killing her. But, when questioned by the police, his brother-in-law denied everything. Police tested the suspect's gun, but its barrel had been **tampered with** and the results were not a match. Investigators needed more evidence.

▲ *Criminalists use an instrument called a gas chromatograph to analyze chemicals in the evidence. From a single vehicle paint chip, machines like this can reveal the make, model, and year of a car!*

Caught By a Hair

The police received a tip that the suspect had thrown two bundles out of his car onto the highway while returning home from Colorado the night of the murder. After a search, the bundles were found. Experts examined one of the suspect's shirts found inside and discovered a hair. Scientific analysis proved the hair belonged to the victim—and the suspect admitted to the murder.

◀ *Experts examine clothes closely for trace evidence such as stains, hairs, and fibers.*

Trace evidence is created when two objects touch each other. It is anything that a criminal leaves behind or takes away from the crime scene. Trace evidence can be visible to the eye or microscopic.

tampered with: deliberately changed

Impression Evidence

Fingerprints are a type of evidence called **impression** evidence. They have often been used to help convict criminals. In 1986, a Washington State man died after taking a pill that contained the poison cyanide. Police suspected the man's wife, but did not have any evidence that linked her to the cyanide. Then they got a tip that the woman had been taking books about poison out of the library. They got her library-card number and found she had borrowed a book called *Deadly Harvest*.

▼ *Impressions at crime scenes can be made by hands, feet, teeth, or vehicle tracks. Tools and weapons also leave impressions.*

Marks on the Page

Police sent the book to the FBI's crime lab. A fingerprint expert lifted 84 prints matching the wife's fingerprints from pages of the book. Most of them were found on the pages dealing with cyanide. The fingerprint impressions helped convince a jury that she was guilty of murdering her husband.

▲ *Impression evidence helped catch and convict*
Ted Bundy, who killed more than 30 people.

Teeth marks are another example of impression evidence. The serial killer Ted Bundy was finally convicted after teeth marks found on a victim matched images of Bundy's teeth.

impression: marks left behind when objects touch one another

Patent and Plastic Fingerprints

Different types of fingerprints are collected in different ways. Patent fingerprints are made by fingertips that are dirty with dust or blood. Plastic impressions are those left in soft surfaces such as sand or wax. Both patent and plastic prints can be seen easily. Forensic experts photograph them, then "lift" them with a special tape.

▲ Experts check for prints on anything the criminal might have touched.

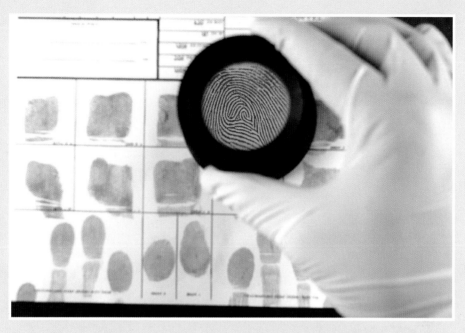

▲ *A fingerprint is the skin tissue that grows on fingertips in whorls, loops, and ridges. Scars from cuts are also part of a fingertip pattern.*

Latent Fingerprints

Latent fingerprints are invisible. These prints are left by sweat and oil from a person's skin. Criminalists dust surfaces at a crime scene with a powder that sticks to the moisture in a fingerprint. The prints can then be photographed and lifted. Experts use a fingerprint **database** to see if the fingerprints found at crime scenes match fingerprints of known criminals.

Since the early 1900s, fingerprint impressions have played the biggest role as evidence to convict criminals. The chances of two people having the same fingerprints are 1 in 64 billion!

database: a collection of information kept on a computer

Footprints

Criminals often arrive at and leave a crime scene quickly. Sometimes they don't take enough time to cover their tracks. This can help criminalists, because tracks from shoes or a vehicle can reveal a lot to experts. Sometimes footprints can be clearly seen in surfaces such as dirt or materials such as sand. They may even be seen in carpets.

Finding Footprints

Even clean, dry shoes leave an impression on surfaces. Electrical charges are created when different materials touch or rub together. These can be seen when fingerprinting dust is sprinkled over them. With the help of special **oblique** lighting, these footprints can be photographed and used as evidence.

◀ *By examining footprints, experts can estimate the height and weight of the criminal.*

Impression casts are made with plaster of Paris or silicone rubber. This material is poured in liquid form into the impression. A model cast is made when the material hardens.

oblique: positioned sideways, or on a slant

Ballistics, Blood, and DNA

Going Ballistic

Firearms leave one-of-a-kind markings on fired **ammunition**. Markings on bullets or bullet casings found at a crime scene can be compared in a ballistics database. This might reveal whether a particular gun has been used in any other crimes.

▲ *The barrel of every gun has a pattern of lines and grooves in it, which leave marks on the shell casing as a bullet is fired.*

Ammunition Evidence

In a 1967 case in Chicago, four bullet casings were found at the crime scene of a woman's murder. The bullets were a very common kind. But ballistics tests showed that they were fired from a special gun called a Walther PPK. A search of the family home revealed a box of the same ammunition with four bullets missing—and a brochure on the Walther PPK locked in the husband's cabinet. The victim's husband was charged with her murder.

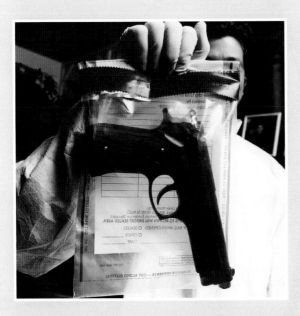

◄ *Ballistics evidence has been used to solve crimes since the 1920s.*

> "Probably the most telling evidence was that the murder was committed with a rare Walther PPK gun like one proved to have been in the possession of defendant earlier that year."

Justice Burt, denying the husband's appeal after he was convicted of murder

ammunition: bullets or shells, which are shot from a weapon

Blood-splatter Analysis

The pattern of a blood-splatter at a crime scene can tell a criminalist a lot. Blood drops that leave a circular shape suggest that the person was not moving during the crime. If that person was closer to the ground, the drops will leave a more round shape. If the person was standing, the blood droplet would have fallen from a greater height, spraying outward in a star-shape.

▲ *Blood-spatter experts can often tell what type of weapon was used in a crime.*

Patterns of Blood

Splashes occur when blood flies through the air and hits a surface at an angle. This usually happens during a struggle, or when someone is hit with a moving weapon. The blood splashes look like exclamation marks (!). Blood spurts show that a lot of blood was pumped from a major **artery** or vein of a victim.

▶ *A blood-splash pattern shows which direction the blood moved in.*

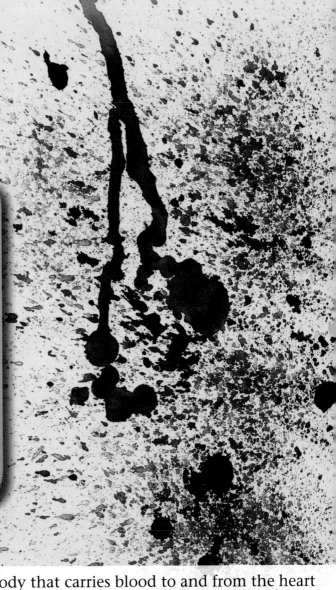

Blood trails show that a bleeding person moved from one place to another. A trail of blood droplets shows that a bleeding body was carried. A smear indicates that a body was dragged.

artery: a tube in the body that carries blood to and from the heart

27

Who Attacked Who?

In 1984, a man whose wife had recently survived an attempted murder, shot and killed his neighbor. The gunman said the neighbor had confessed to him that he was the one who had tried to kill his wife. He claimed to have shot the victim in **self-defense** because he had attacked him with a knife. He had bloody slashes on his own chest and face to prove it. But something did not add up for investigators.

▶ *Round drops reveal that an injury took place while the victim was not moving.*

Blood Tells the True Story

A criminalist studied the blood splatter—and it told a different story. The drops of blood from the gunman fell in a round shape. This meant that he had been standing still when slashed, not fighting for his life against a knife attack. Also, the gun that killed the victim had no blood on it, even though the killer was covered in blood! Blood evidence proved that the surviving neighbor had cut himself *after* murdering the victim. In the end, investigators determined he had tried to kill his own wife for the insurance, blamed it on the neighbor, and shot him to cover it up.

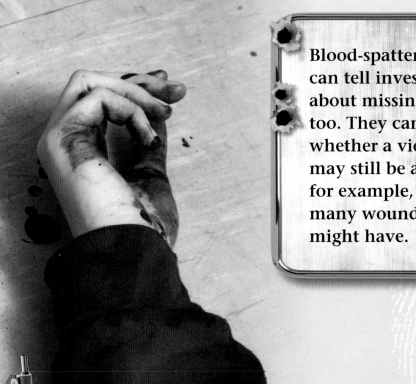

Blood-spatter analysts can tell investigators about missing victims, too. They can say whether a victim may still be alive, for example, or how many wounds they might have.

self-defense: fighting back when someone attacks you first

DNA Discovered

DNA (deoxyribonucleic acid) is the string of genetic code found in the cells of living things. In 1984, British scientist Alec Jeffreys realized that the pattern of DNA code was different in every person—except identical twins. He had established the world's first genetic fingerprint. A few years later, DNA was first used to help solve a crime.

▼ *Dr. Alec Jeffreys showed how DNA could be used in forensic science.*

DNA Fingerprinting

Jeffreys went on to create **techniques** for DNA fingerprinting (also called DNA profiling). A DNA sample can be found in body tissues or fluids such as saliva, sweat, and blood. DNA is removed from the sample and tested in forensic laboratories. DNA databases, such as CODIS, are used to identify suspects in a crime.

◀ *Special computer programs reveal the pattern of a person's DNA—their "DNA fingerprint"— which looks a bit like a barcode.*

CODIS stands for Combined DNA Index System. Managed by the FBI, this is a program that gathers together and shares DNA information from crime scenes all over the country. It stores profiles on millions of offenders, allowing investigators to check their forensic findings against a central database.

techniques: ways of doing something to get a certain result

A Lack of Evidence

When a 60-year-old Connecticut woman was found strangled in 1998, police immediately had a suspect. The caretaker for the building where the woman went to the laundromat had previously been to prison for assault. The suspect's cousin, also suspicious of him, took the car his cousin had been borrowing to the police. Criminalists searched the car and found biological evidence, but DNA tests at the time could not link the caretaker to the crime.

The Clue on the Cigarettes

Ten years went by, but investigators did not give up. By this time, the science of DNA testing was more advanced. They sent the evidence in for testing again. This time forensic experts matched DNA from the saliva on the suspect's cigarettes with DNA from the **duct tape** that had been used to tie the victim up. This was the long-awaited proof police needed to charge their suspect with murder.

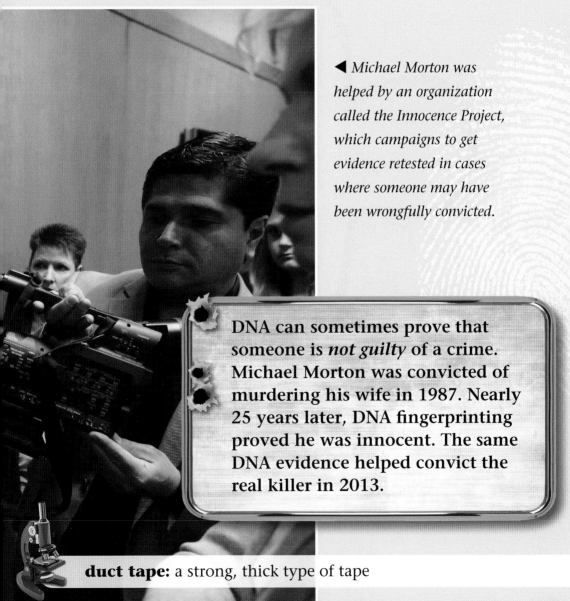

◀ *Michael Morton was helped by an organization called the Innocence Project, which campaigns to get evidence retested in cases where someone may have been wrongfully convicted.*

DNA can sometimes prove that someone is *not guilty* of a crime. Michael Morton was convicted of murdering his wife in 1987. Nearly 25 years later, DNA fingerprinting proved he was innocent. The same DNA evidence helped convict the real killer in 2013.

duct tape: a strong, thick type of tape

Arson and Explosives

Burning Evidence

During the 1980s and 1990s, there were several fires at businesses in California. Four people died and the fires caused millions of dollars of damage. Investigators discovered that the fires were caused by **accelerants** and explosive devices set off by timers. Strangely, some of the fires happened near where arson investigators' conferences were taking place!

SHERIFF'S LINE DO NOT CROSS

▲ *Arson investigators search crime scenes where fires have been for evidence such as impressions, physical evidence, and accelerants.*

Investigator-Turned-Arsonist

After one of the fires, a fingerprint was found on a piece of paper inside an explosive device. Police ran the print through their database, but it did not match any known criminal. Investigators took fingerprints from arson experts attending the nearby conferences—and one of them matched. The head of an arson unit had actually started the fires.

▲ *Sometimes dogs are specially trained to help investigators find the fire's point of origin.*

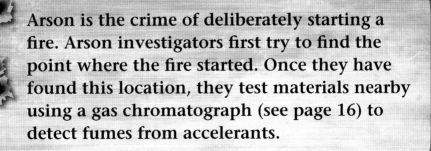

Arson is the crime of deliberately starting a fire. Arson investigators first try to find the point where the fire started. Once they have found this location, they test materials nearby using a gas chromatograph (see page 16) to detect fumes from accelerants.

accelerants: fuels that make a fire start quickly and burn hotter

The Lockerbie Bomb

On December 21, 1988, a bomb destroyed a passenger plane while it was flying over Lockerbie, Scotland. The bomb killed all 259 people on the plane, plus 11 more on the ground. Experts set to work figuring out who had committed this terrible crime.

▼ *The wreckage of the plane was spread over an area of about 1,000 square miles (2,590 square kilometers).*

Putting the Pieces Together

Criminalists managed to collect about 90 percent of the wreckage. It took many months for experts to reconstruct the plane. But when it was done, investigators discovered exactly where the bomb had been when it exploded. By examining the extent of the damage in certain places, they knew where it was in the luggage compartment. By finding the pieces, they even knew the color and make of the suitcase it was hidden in. Investigators eventually determined that the bomb had been planted by terrorists from Libya.

Explosives scatter a blanket of explosive chemical **residue** over an area. Criminalists collect samples of this residue from the scene of the crime, and put it in containers that are specially made to preserve the evidence.

residue: tiny bits that remain after a process has finished

Computer Catches a Killer

A serial killer murdered ten people in Kansas from 1974 to 1991. He **taunted** the police by sending letters and packages to them and to the media. In these letters, he included details and photographs of his murders. He also included personal items that belonged to his victims. DNA testing at the time was still very new.

Digital forensic experts use something called a "write blocker" to find information on computer hard drives. Write blockers prove that digital information was not changed in any way during the investigation.

The Disk Trail

In a letter to the police in 2005, the killer asked if they could trace his letters if he sent them on a floppy disk. Police responded in a newspaper ad that they could not. But digital forensics experts could, in fact, trace disks. The next letter came on a floppy disk and was traced to a computer at the Christ Lutheran Church in Wichita. The church council's president was arrested and sentenced to ten consecutive life sentences.

▼ *The judge reads the charges to the serial killer, who appeared in court via a video link. He was eventually convicted of all ten murders.*

taunted: deliberately made someone angry

Cyber Crime

Before the 1990s, very few people had personal computers. Today, many people use the Internet through computers, tablets, and cell phones. This technology has given rise to a new type of crime—**cyber** attacks. Cyber attacks are crimes that are committed through computers or computer networks such as the Internet.

▲ *Cyber crimes include identity theft and credit-card fraud. Governments fear that cyber spies will steal top-secret information!*

Going Digital

Digital forensics is the science of finding evidence from digital devices such as computers, cell phones, security cameras, and other digital devices. Digital forensics experts find evidence from digital devices used by criminals. Even emails, texts, or Internet histories that have been deleted can be retrieved by these criminalists.

▲ *The FBI's Computer Analysis Response Team (CART) recovers information from digital devices. They testify in court on their findings.*

"A savvy investigator with the right tools can fairly easily reconstruct information that the user thought had been deleted."

David Stenhouse, computer investigator at Seattle's University of Washington

cyber: relating to computer networks such as the Internet

A Computerized World

Computer technology has changed the way forensic scientists discover, process, and test evidence. Before computers, criminalists had the time-consuming job of looking through information recorded on paper documents. Today, they use computers to instantly search databases and compare information all over the world.

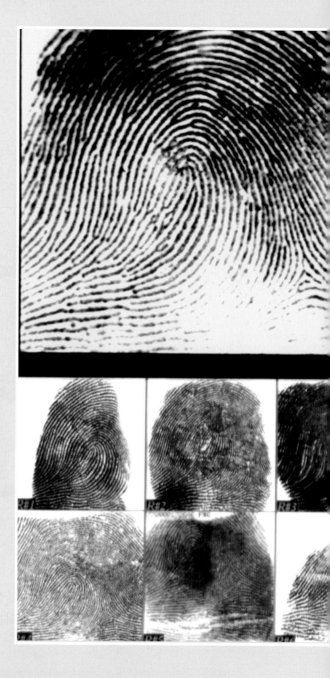

▶ *Today, finding and comparing evidence such as fingerprints or a person's DNA, is easier, faster, and more reliable than ever.*

The Royal Canadian Mounted Police first stored fingerprint records in computer databases in 1973. By the 1990s, tens of thousands of these records could be compared every second.

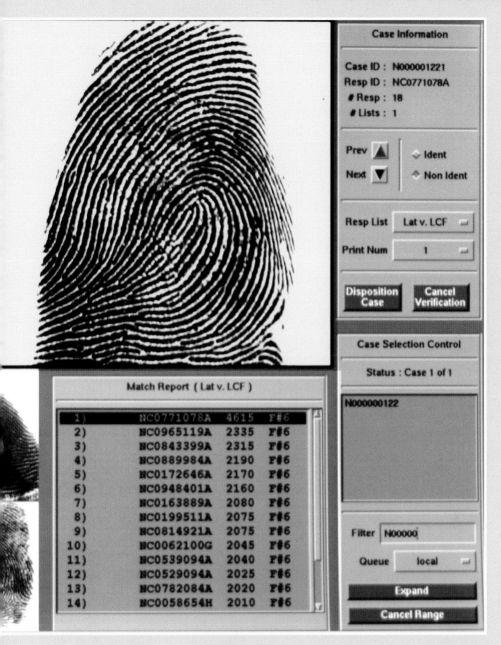

Case Information

Case ID : N000001221
Resp ID : NC0771078A
Resp : 18
Lists : 1

Prev ▲   ◇ Ident

Next ▼   ◇ Non Ident

Resp List   Lat v. LCF

Print Num   1

Disposition Case   Cancel Verification

Case Selection Control

Status : Case 1 of 1

N000000122

Filter   N00000

Queue   local

Expand

Cancel Range

Match Report (Lat v. LCF)

1)	NC0771078A	4615	F#6
2)	NC0965119A	2335	F#6
3)	NC0843399A	2315	F#6
4)	NC0889984A	2190	F#6
5)	NC0172646A	2170	F#6
6)	NC0948401A	2160	F#6
7)	NC0163889A	2080	F#6
8)	NC0199511A	2075	F#6
9)	NC0814921A	2075	F#6
10)	NC0062100G	2045	F#6
11)	NC0539094A	2040	F#6
12)	NC0529094A	2025	F#6
13)	NC0782084A	2020	F#6
14)	NC0058654H	2010	F#6

Artificial Intelligence

The FBI created a computer system with **artificial intelligence**, which they called Floyd. Floyd's database holds the FBI's top-secret collection of information about crimes and criminals. Investigating agents use Floyd to help them search for possible suspects.

artificial intelligence: computers that think like humans

The "CSI Effect"

Crime-scene investigation shows, such as *CSI: Crime Scene Investigation*, have made forensics a wildly popular subject. Because of these shows, many more young people are studying sciences at college and choosing a career as a criminalist. This has been nicknamed the "CSI Effect."

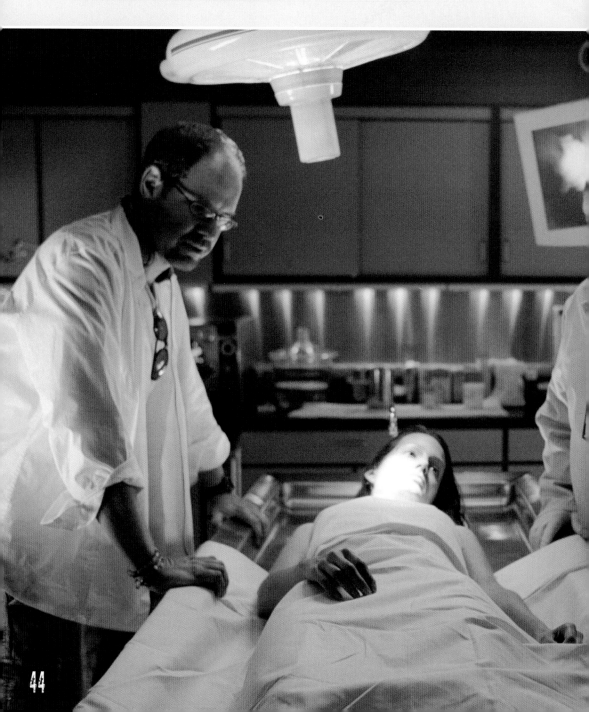

TV World vs. Real World

What you see on TV is not always true to life. Sometimes the forensic technologies seen on these shows are not yet available in real life. Wait times for test results are also much longer than they seem to be on TV. Despite this, advances in forensic science have undoubtedly helped to catch and convict criminals who never would have been caught 30 years ago.

◀ *The "CSI Effect" is a term used to describe how crime-scene investigation television shows influence people's ideas about forensics.*

White fibers found at crime scenes are often ignored by CSIs because they are so common they don't give enough information. But a new technique using X-ray photoelectron spectroscopy (XPS) could change this. The new method uses X-rays to reveal chemicals on the surface of the fiber. This may tell experts whether the material has been treated to make it stain-**resistant** or iron-free, for example, which could narrow the search.

resistant: able to withstand something

Learning More

Books

Crime Lab Detectives (Amazing Crime Scene Science)
by John Townsend
(Amicus, 2011)

Forensic Evidence: Prints
(Crabtree Contact)
by John Townsend
(Crabtree Publishing, 2008)

Forensic Evidence: Blood
(Crabtree Contact)
by Darlene Stille
(Crabtree Publishing, 2008)

Forensic Science (Cool Science)
by Ron Fridell
(Lerner Books, 2008)

Zoom in on Crime Scenes
by Richard Spilsbury
(Enslow Publishers, 2013)

Websites

www.fbi.gov/fun-games/ kids/kids
The FBI's "kids page," which includes information about investigative techniques

www.fbi.gov/news/ stories/2013/january/piecing-together-digital-evidence/ piecing-together-digital-evidence
Information about the FBI Computer Analysis Response Team (CART)

http://kidsahead.com/ subjects/3-forensics/activities
Forensics activities for kids

http://www.2learn.ca/kids/ listSciG6.aspx?Type=59
An "Evidence and Investigation" page, with links to information and activities about CSI and forensics.

Glossary

accelerants Fuels that make a fire start quickly and burn hotter

ammunition Bullets or shells, which are shot from a weapon

animation Pictures or graphics that seem to show movement

artery A tube in the body that carries blood to and from the heart

artificial intelligence Computers that think like humans

ballistics The scientific study of bullets and firearms

contaminate Change something so it is no longer reliable evidence

cyber Relating to computer networks such as the Internet

database A collection of information kept on a computer

duct tape A strong, thick type of tape

forensic A scientific way to solve a crime

impression Marks left behind when objects touch one another

investigate Look into something to discover the truth

latex A material from plants that is used to make a type of rubber

oblique Positioned sideways, or on a slant

residue Tiny bits that remain after a process has finished

resistant Able to withstand something

self-defense Fighting back when someone attacks you first

tampered with Deliberately changed

taunted Deliberately made someone angry

techniques Ways of doing something to get a certain result

Index

Entries in **bold** refer to pictures